Why

To Be Your Brother's Keeper

Arthur Jerome Bott Sr.

Printed by Createspace

Created and published through Arthur Jerome Bott Sr.

Printed in the United States of America

Book edited and designed by Maria Erazo Enterprises
For more information about Maria Erazo Enterprises publisher
Visit: www.mariaerazo.com

ISBN: 978-0-692-09088-6

Table of Contents

Forward

Kate Davis: Senior Director of Advancement Operations, and Annual Giving at Aquinas College.

Art Bott attended Aquinas College and attributed his relationship with its founders, the Dominican Sisters ~ Grand Rapids to be a vital part of his development as a young adult and eventual leader. In my work at Aquinas, I've had many conversations and communications with Art about his passion for Catholic education, the significance of the College to him and the community, and his enduring commitment to lifelong leadership. As a benefactor to the College, Art has worked with me closely to ensure that his legacy is present on campus so that it may inspire current and future students, faculty, staff, and guests.

Art is a generous leader and advisor to the Catholic community of West Michigan. He is a true entrepreneur, having started numerous companies and supporting many business ventures. He has a strong feeling that his calling is to create pathways to job success to the community. He is well-known and respected not only as a leader but also a partner. He often says, "Attitude and gratitude will lead a person to success," a motto that he lives. He has a particular interest in preserving historical buildings and beautification of communities.

Art's well-known for his generous post-retirement intervention at Grand Rapids Plastics, where he literally rescued the company and its 400 employees. At Aquinas, he is a generous friend who made possible the St. Thomas Aquinas Entry Court and numerous improvements to our historical buildings and gardens. He has helped so many of our students who enjoy our athletics facilities, residence halls, and Cook carriage house which houses our student organizations. Additionally, he supports programming for students in more ways than I can name.

The theme of Art's life is that faith, perseverance, and hard work pay off in so many ways. Art is a talented businessman, but more importantly, he is a kind, selfless man who developed, by necessity, a strong work ethic at a very early age. Throughout his life, he has honored God and sought ways to help others. He is, indeed a transformational leader.

Forward

Gaspar Ancona

Arthur Bott has been a friend of mine since I became pastor of St. Sebastian Church in Byron Center, Michigan, in 1994. At the time, St. Sebastian's was a little country church on Wilson Avenue in the midst of corn fields. It had a long and proud history, beginning with German immigrants who settled in the area and began to farm the fields. The parish numbered 160 families when I arrived. Now, it has an additional large church, beautifully set behind the historic little church on increased acreage, with a membership nearing 1000 families.

Before my assignment to St. Sebastian's, I had been Rector of the Cathedral of St. Andrew located in downtown Grand Rapids for ten years. I had also been a writer for the diocesan periodicals, and a radio panelist on the weekly ecumenical program called "Soundings." Bishop Robert J. Rose assigned me to St. Sebastian's as pastor, with the added request that I research and write the history of the diocese of Grand Rapids. The Bishop thought that the parish size and location would afford me the time for such an extra assignment.

Arthur was a parishioner at St. Sebastian's and had built a lovely home in Railside. Before long, I visited him in his home, as I did other parishioners, and came to enjoy his friendship. At Christmas time, I remember how he opened his home to the senior adults of the parish for parties and the singing together of favorite Christmas hymns.

Arthur did not grow up with wealth. Because of his youthful experience as a caddy, he became unusually skilled at the game of golf, won school scholarships, and entered the business world. His success as an entrepreneur was not without setbacks, but with determination, he set himself on track again and again. It is this kind of persevering that has served Arthur Bott and his endeavors so well in many areas of life. His family upbringing and religious faith have been the bedrock for the achievements that came later in his life. They also served to strengthen him and his resolve during the times of challenge.

Arthur has delighted in being the successful channel for others to make a living, raise their families, and achieve their life goals. He has always been especially proud to be able to provide minorities within our society the opportunity to work and enjoy the fruits of their labor. Working at these goals is what Arthur Bott has seen as a fulfilling life for a Catholic Christian businessman.

Rev. Msgr. Gaspar F. Ancona

Pastor Emeritus of St. Sebastian Church, Byron Center, Michigan

March 2018

Forward

My name is Monsignor William H. Duncan, and I am a Catholic priest, pastor of Saint Sebastian Church in Byron Center, MI. I have known Art for approx. 20 years. Meeting him through a Catholic businessman's association and then serving as the pastor of the parish where he attends. I am aware of Art's professional credentials as a values-driven successful manufacturing executive. He cared deeply about his employees especially those he could hire who had fallen on hard times and needed a second chance at a job. Art's faith is the source of his kindness, generosity, and desire to help others. Many lives have been impacted by the commitment to others over these many years.

Sincerely yours,

Msgr. Duncan

Forward

Mary Waller- general manager for Brownwood Acres Foods

I met Art through my Mom who dated him in college. Art swept in and reconnected with my Mom over 60 years later. At the time my Mom now had dementia. He visited her and talked to her like a normal Individual which helped her tremendously. He even took her on vacation to her father's retirement center in Florida for ten days (no easy task)

I think Art's lower beginning and faith in God will inspire others never to give up. Through hard work and faith in our Lord, you can achieve anything.

Forward

My name is Ali Izzet Erhan.

My current full-time job is Development manager at Advansys Engineering Services Company, but I also teach economics at GRCC since 1995. I started teaching Fall of 1986

I met Art at Sunrise Rotary Club when we were both charter members. We continue our friendship ever since. He is a wonderful person. Caring, helpful, sharing, etc… He has a great attitude towards life, and he appreciates everything he has. Two words cover his life. Attitude and Gratitude.

Art always had a great approach to life. He lived true Christian faith. He knew that all of us are temporary in this world and the real owner was God. We are only a steward of things were trusted to us. He worked many years without getting paid a single dime at Grand Rapids Plastics. He worked very hard to provide employment. He did it all for his employees and family. He could have retired in Florida and enjoy his time, but he put people before him.

He was very generous with his support of educational institutions also. His legacy at Aquinas College and MSU exceed himself. He spent many years at Rotary International helping local and international projects also. He has been a mentor to me.

Acknowledgement

I am forever grateful for Divine Intervention. To John and Sue Teeples who generously gave me the gift of the life of his Kidney as a living donor. I want to acknowledge my parents for the love and guidance they provide it for me, and for keeping me within my boundaries. I want to thank my sister, Virginia Bott Warner, for my old time favorite sister. To the Dominican sisters at St. Alphonsus' Catholic Central High School. To William M Broucek for never losing faith in me. To my five children for calling me Dad. To Dan Brink for being a golfing buddy and my High School teammates James Black, Dan Pupel, Jim Sullivan, and the Aquinas College and Michigan State University..

To the various employees and business partners that allowed me to be a part of their lives. To the people that help me earn the Lifetime achievement award. And the skilled trades people that made it possible for my home in Byron Center be the home of the year thanked you for the input and skilled in building a house that was built 25 years ahead of its time.

To James P Bouwman for his financial support, leadership and for treating me like a younger brother. To Bill Broucek for your guidance and financial support, you two are the ones that indeed made a difference in my personal life.

Chapter One

What Is Success?

No one wants to be a failure; everyone wants to succeed. These desires are reflected in the mass amount of self-help literature, programs, and lecturers all claiming they can teach people how to become successful. But most of these resources provide conflicting information, making it difficult to know which ones are trustworthy and which ones are propaganda. Part of the confusion is the very definition of success. Merriam-Webster defines "success" as the attainment of a "favorable or desirable outcome." If that's the case, then the meaning of success varies from person to person. So, if you haven't already, it's time to ask yourself how you define success.

Throughout our lives, we experience eye-opening moments. It's as though a heavy fog has lifted, and we can finally navigate our way back to common sense. These experiences make life a bit easier and the load a little lighter.

I had just transferred from civil engineering to the school of packaging at Michigan State when I had my own moment of awakening. I was sitting in a classroom listening to a lecture when I realized that this is all I had ever done. I'd been lectured my whole life. All of us, we're told what to do before we even take our first steps. In reality, I don't think I retained even 10% of what I was supposed to learn in college, because college doesn't teach you life's most important and memorable lessons. You learn more from experience than you do from lectures. I earned my diploma from Michigan State, but my real degree is from the college of hard knocks.

In every seminar, conference, and meeting I've attended for business, everyone's lecturing. Everyone's telling you what to do and how to do it. You can't even ask questions—you're just supposed to sit there and listen. But when you can't ask questions, you can't engage. I thought that perhaps this was a key component I had been missing in my own business and relationships with clients. When we needed to be having open, two-way dialogue, I had been boring them with one-way sales pitches. I wanted to start engaging my clients and I knew that were only possible if I started asking questions, listening, and learning. Asking questions meant I had stopped pushing product that people may not necessarily even want. From endeavoring to merely turn a profit, my business became an enterprise selling people what they need. Asking questions transformed typical consumer/supplier interactions into real relationships. I trusted my clients and they trusted me.

Questions help others feel included instead of excluded. Participative conversation and participative management gets everyone involved. People are more responsive to someone who isn't a know-it-all. My mother taught me the phrase, "big mouth, no brains," about people who talked as if they knew everything about everything. That type of attitude turns people off. But by asking questions, you let others know you're aware that you don't have all the answers. Questions indicate that you can trust others to provide some answers, that you respect their intellect and believe in them.

Education is vital to our growth and success—and questions provide that education. Not everyone can be a carpenter. Not everyone is cut out for business and sales. Only a select few can be brain surgeons. No one is skilled in everything. Each person has a different calling to fulfill in this life. But there is one, universal purpose shared by everyone. Every single one of us must figure out what we have to do in order to leave this world a little better than the way it was when we got here.

Nothing in this life lasts forever and nothing is meant to stay the same. Change is natural and healthy, and the absence of change is a sign of poor condition and decay. Think of a lively river and how the water is constantly moving, carrying with it fish and plant life. Now, picture stagnant water, its foul and rancid smell, the skin of film that has formed on the surface as bacteria has grown unchecked and rampantly. That water is filthy and undrinkable, and it will eventually evaporate under the sun. Whether it's a turn of events, a career switch, a new development within our personal relationships, many people fear change. But the world cannot improve if it doesn't change.

We must do whatever we can to help others. Wealth shouldn't be flaunted in the faces of people who don't have it. It should be shared. These things don't change overnight, and so we have to begin with our children. Elementary students should be learning more than sentence structure and multiplication. Learning to use kind words, how to talk to each other, and how to be more empathetic—these, too, are lessons our children need. From a young age, people should be taught how to civilly resolve disagreements, solve problems, and work together.

I was blessed with parents who raised me to be grateful. They taught me how to be kind and to always lend a helping hand to those in need. Unfortunately, not everyone is as lucky as I was. Not everyone grows up in a healthy and loving environment. This is why we need a curriculum of values in our schools. Grades can't be the only measure of a child's success. Children need to be taught about human nature, empathy, and what it means to be a good person. Churches could better benefit others if they preached less about these values and demonstrated them instead. They should strive to create a following by leading through example. Getting into the habit of giving is perhaps the hardest thing in the world for some people to do. But when churches give, its members learn to give.

All of today's problems are in one way or another caused by selfishness. Entirely too concerned with themselves, most people won't do anything without first asking, "What's in it for me?" If we could get people to alter their thinking and redirect their attention onto others instead of focusing on themselves, we would solve nearly all of the world's problems. If people would start giving more than they take, then the needs of every person would be met. Think of the impact it would have on crime. Prisons aren't full of givers, because people in prison didn't have anything to give in the first place. No one resorts to a life of crime because they think it's fun. People steal, sell drugs, and commit identity theft because their primary needs aren't being met.

I am not a socialist and I do not propose a kind of system where wealth is distributed evenly throughout society. Something, however, does need to change. There shouldn't be people working 40 hours a week or more and yet have to frequently choose between paying the light bill and feeding their children. If there was a national endeavor to change the way we earn, spend, and save our money, suicide rates would decline drastically. When people are suffering from grief, mental illness, or trauma, financial trouble is often the thing that pushes them over the edge.

I've been asked by many people what it takes to be a millionaire. The answer is simple. I tell them to stop any and all senseless spending. Impulse buying wastes your money. Concentrate on your interpersonal relationships rather than on material goods. This way you'll find that you not only have more money in your pocket, but greater peace as well.

It keeps coming back to answering the question, "Why are you here?" It's not an answer that anyone easily comes by, it's something you have to soul search for. You can't blame others when things go wrong. There's only one person who can change you, and that's you. And you can't make someone else change by lecturing them.

When you're out and about, take notice and observe those around you. If you're at the grocery and you see someone ask the cashier to take out some of the items they intended to purchase, why not step up and buy it all for them? Acts of kindness are more important than what you buy materially for yourself. Once you buy something for yourself, the rush is over. On top of that, you have to maintain it as well. It owns you. Things you own only waste your time, your talent, and your financial resources. But there is no greater feeling than the one you receive from giving. When you give to others, everybody wins.

Now that we know how important questions are, I have some questions for you. Feel free to write your answers directly onto this page. This book is an autobiography, yes. But I also want you to think of it like a kind of workbook.

How do you define success? What would you need to accomplish in order to call yourself successful?

____

____

____

Why are you here? What talents do you possess that you know to be unique to you? What things do you do best?

____

____

____

____

How can you use these talents to benefit others?

____

____

____

____

When was the last time you helped someone in need?

____

____

____

____

When was the last time you witnessed someone in need and didn't help them?

____

____

____

____

Chapter Two

Who Am I?

On April 18, 1934, I was born during the Great Depression in Grand Rapids, Michigan at St. Mary's hospital. At a time when most people were unemployed, my father, Jerome Alfred Bott, didn't have a job either. And like most wives and mothers in those days, she was a stay home mother, although she was educated.

When I was born, my parents had an apartment on Spencer and Union on the upper floor. That's where we lived while my father remained unemployed throughout the Depression. Eventually, my mother got him a job as a beer truck-driver for the Grand Rapids Brewery on the west side of town. From his modest salary, my parents saved their money and bought our first house at 1625 North Avenue Northeast. It was just two houses south of Creston High School. The homes there were set close together and it was maybe the size of a stall and a half garage. We had a coal furnace and an ice box. Milk was delivered directly to the house. We also had a telephone that was on a party line. The neighbors were all very neighborly. None of us had any money. We passed clothes up and down the street, and the bulk of us prayed together because most were members of St. Alphonsus between Lafayette and Leonard Street. The focal point of our life was religion.

My younger sister, Virginia Anita Bott, was born on March 1, 1937. She is in all of my fondest childhood memories. Close in age, we were playmates. We went to shows together, played with the other neighborhood kids—all kinds of games that didn't cost money. We had to follow certain guidelines but it was still a wonderful time of life – much better than now.

My mother, Leona Helen Yost (also pronounced Jost) was born Alpine Township, in the Comstock /Alpine area on Peach Ridge. Her side of the family had a big garden, and we lived off its vegetables and fruit for years until my father got a new job at Fox Deluxe brewery, which was on Michigan Street between Ionia and Ottawa. He worked there until the brewery closed after the Second World War.

My dad became the president of the Beer and Soft Drink Union. Born at home in Remus, Michigan in 1905, my father wasn't verbally loving, but he was strong and devoted. He was firm. If my sister and I were loud while he read the paper, he would shake it once. If we didn't calm down, he would shake it a second time. You didn't want him to shake it a third time, because he had the fastest belt in Grand Rapids. None of us wanted to have the belt. As soon as he started to unbuckle it, we quietened down.

I have carried on these family traditions with my own children. For me, the most wonderful word in the English language is "Dad." To be called Dad meant a great deal to me Being a single parent of five kids, I gave them guidelines to follow. There was 20% responsibility for each one of them. We were co-dependent on each other. Sharing responsibility was part of being a family. I could take the kids out for dinner and they would be little ladies and gentlemen. I could line all five of them up on a pew at mass. Good manners and behavior start with parenting. If parents are confused and don't know what they're doing, that is passed along to the children. But if parents are quiet and in control, their kids are too because it's all they know. The parent has to set the example, because the bulk of what is learned in life begins at home.

Today, most relationships have been replaced with material items. But I grew up watching my mother and father love each other. There was peace between them. As a family, we didn't have all the distractions that there are today. My family and I listened and saw it on the radio. We played board games such as Monopoly and Sorry. But our favorite game was Cribbage. All mental competition and concentration, it was a battle of who could answer questions the fastest. We took family trips too, and we enjoyed the car rides along the way. One Sunday each month, we would all go to Alpine and have dinner with relatives out there. The next Sunday, we would go to Remus where we would spend the day with my father's 10 brothers and two sisters. It looked like we were holding a convention when we went up there. My sister and I played with all the cousins and the women would cook.

I was easily distracted as a kid. The principal called my mother in for a conference one day when I was in the fifth grade. My mother never learned to drive, so she walked a couple of miles to the principal's office at St. Alphonsus for that conference.

The principal, a Dominican Nun, told my mother that I would never amount to anything. My mother said to her, "You just wait and see. I have a lot to say about this, and I'm not giving up on this kid." There's no difference between a father's love and a mother's love. Love is love. Growing up, I was closer to my mother than I was to my father. My dad was stern with me, but he was a softy when it came to my sister. Over time, I found that it's normal for most girls to be closer to their fathers and most boys to be closer to their mothers. Because I was closer to my mother, I had more guidance from her. She was an inspiration through many of the trials in my young life. My mother was my greatest advocate. A genuinely kind woman, I still consider her the smartest person I've ever known. She was brilliant. In fact, schooling was so important to her that she stayed at the YWCA so she could attend Catholic Central on Sheldon Avenue in downtown Grand Rapids. She had a two-year college education. And she made my education a priority. And then she went to Sacred Heart College for two years which was newly funded by the Dominican nuns, and eventually became Aquinas College as it is today.

One of my biggest challenges during my youth was dealing with the brutalities of bullies. People were cruel to my family because we were German. During WWII they treated us like we were Nazis. There were lots of bullies in school, and having never been a violent person, I was small and scared of them. They would hit me and say mean things to me. For example, because my name was Art, they would say stuff like, "Art let a fart all the way to John Ball Park." I was mocked a lot because of my stuttering. We all know we're not perfect by any means, but when your imperfections are right out in front of you, you can't hide them. My imperfection was out there to be criticized every time I opened my mouth. The unfortunate part was that there wasn't any help to correct my speech.

The fact I had a stutter didn't mean I lacked common sense. I had vision and a good head on my shoulders, but I didn't perform as academically well as my mother would've liked to see. Conventional education has a cookie cutter approach. One education for all. Too much time and attention is given to earning high grades instead of developing a child's individual skills. We must do a better job of supporting our youth by finding out how their minds uniquely think. We must help them concentrate on the positive and eliminate the negative. Education, so often, emphasizes weaknesses instead of improving upon strengths.

Growing up with a stuttering problem actually removed me from that patterned education and furthered my concentration and focus. It helped me find myself so I would know which direction to take in life. Conquering my stutter required that I put my thought in line. It was a process of elimination. In other words, if you don't try, you don't know. I was self-taught. I had to be my own best friend because I was talking to myself all the time.

My self-esteem was low, and the only way I found to boost it was playing golf. I think caddying shaped my life when I was a child. When you're poor, you're treated like you're poor and people who had money, especially their children, were cruel to poor people. When I was caddying at Kent Country Club, I worked for the blue bloods. But mingling with them, even as a caddy, made me feel that we were no different.

The cruelties were demeaning. Most people want to see you fail because they, themselves, feel like failures. Instead of trying to lift you up, they criticize everything about you. Even the nuns who taught at my school were like that.

Few people teach through kindness and understanding. Instead of analyzing each one of their students to discover their individual capabilities, working on the positive instead of trying to find fault or criticizing students because of a certain grade, some teachers exercise their own will. It's nasty.

I think schooling is a matter of what you need to be a better person and how to accelerate the gifts you have been given in life. In a nation of younger people who can play up to the teachers and who have their cliques as a power base, someone who wants to be alone so they can meditate can't be themselves. So, they have to find the right environment to be alone. My environment was on the golf course. When I was out there, I was in my safe haven. I felt protected when practicing on that golf course at night, getting the lay of the greens by walking around barefoot. I learned how to win on the course by working on my short game. Instead of spending time hitting the ball, I became a skilled putter.

Although life is complicated, it is also an interesting and beautiful experience. Because you have all these outside influences from other people, places and things that want to control your life. My happiest days were going through grade school and high school. I learned about life, competitiveness and different ways of living. I wasn't born again, as many people describe it. I prefer to say that I woke up.

Being born again is a learning process as you grow. You finally get to a point where you really think of yourself as a person. I had the foundation of my youth at home to draw from. My roots continued to deepen and fortify as I grew older.

That type of foundation is missing in today's society. I think the worst thing that happened to this country was World War II. While the men were at war, the women had to work. They continued to work outside the home even after the men returned from war. Not having a parent at home with the children has harmed our country. Someone has to be home to know what's going on during the day.

So, you have all of this deepness, all of these things that are going on. And where do you go? There's no place to go. We really have to understand why we're here. We're here because we have a role to play.

Think about everything that you see today. You see all the things that go on, the self-serving. Divine Intervention is important. When God calls, you better answer the phone. You really have to think and listen because you don't know anything. And part of life is being able to ask for help, asking God for help and guidance. "I don't know what I'm doing. Help me. It's Thy will. What do you want me to do with my life?"

So what has God called you to do? If you don't know the answer to this question, that's okay. I am going to provide some prompts and steps here to help you arrive at a conclusion.

#1. Think about your parents. Think about a piece of advice they gave you that has stuck with you through your life? Even if you didn't have the best mother and father, I'm sure they taught you something—even if it was accidental and you learned a valuable life lesson by watching them make their own mistakes. Now, think of a way you can apply their advice or life lesson to your life today.

How can you apply a lesson you learned from your parents to your life TODAY? What kinds of things would that lesson improve?

____

____

____

____

#2. Think back to last chapter where you named your talents. It could be one specific thing you're good at, or even several different things. Now, think about how you could use those to help others. Forget about turning a profit for a while. After all, in order to turn a profit you must have something to offer.

Considering one of your talents, how can you use it to help others?

____
____
____
____

#3. Reflect upon the times people have helped you. Think of one example, and think of how you would've been without the help of that person. Would you have made it without them? Odds are, yes, you would've. But when people help each other, it restores our faith in humanity and trust in our neighbors.

What did it mean to you when you were helped by someone else? How would your life look differently if they had never helped you? How can you make an impact on the life of someone else just as you were impacted?

____
____
____
____

Chapter Three

Golf

When I was growing up during the Great Depression, I listened to the voices of the poor. I listened to the news. Health problems were the biggest struggles families faced at that time. My mother, for example, had a ruptured appendix when I was in the fifth grade, and there wasn't any penicillin. Hospitalized for six months, my sister stayed with our neighbor Margaret Moleski, a friend of my mother's. I stayed with my Aunt Bernice and Uncle Harry.

I've worked all my life. I worked on the family farm from the time I was very young. And because of all the work I've done, I've been exposed to many different kinds of people. It's important for young people to spend time around their elders. Being around older, more successful people, I learned from them as I determined what it was that stood out about each of them. I would be working three or four feet away from these people, and I'd think, "Oh, I like that approach." They'd forget I was there, so I was kind of like a mouse in the church that hears more confessions than the priest

In 1942, I was eight years old, and World War II was still raging. My family was poor at the time, and I knew I wanted to get ahead and make something of myself. So, I went up to Kent Country Club and asked if I could caddy. I knew nothing of golf, but I got the nine holes anyway. A.G. Dickenson, who owned Dickenson Printing, hired me. His bag as big as I was, I had to drag it from hole to hole. Mr. Dickenson paid me 75 cents, and I thought I was rich.

At that point, I became interested in golf and got a hold of a wooden shaft to practice with. I think it might have been a niblick, which is the antiquated term for a nine iron. The shafts were all wooden at that time, so clubs were called spoons, niblicks, and other names. I particularly enjoyed playing golf because of my stuttering problem. The only way I could find some peace was to be active. I could play golf all by myself. I didn’t have to talk to anyone. I could just practice and improve a little more day by day, building up my self-esteem along the way.

Kent Country Club allowed their caddies to play golf for free on Mondays. We used clubs that belonged to the club’s members, so I never knew what kind of clubs I would have to work with. To advance my skills, I read Ben

Hogan's book, *Power Golf*, and studied what the game was all about. Much of the text discussed the shorter parts of the game. Because just like in life everything means something, every decision takes you somewhere—in golf, each stroke is significant.

At night, I would go over to Kent Country Club and practice those little things that upgraded my game. There was a security guard there that I called Pete the Cop. He would come after me and I would run as fast as I could, slipping and sliding across the green to escape him. I'd return, and Pete the Cop would come after me again. He eventually grew tired of chasing me off the green and he began to walk around with me instead. I used to go from green to green with my handkerchief in the dark and practice putting instead of hitting the ball. I would place my feet at the exact level the putt needed to be. Most people don't realize that they're hands and their feet are the most sensitive parts of the body. They transmit everything.

My game continued to improve as I aged. In the eighth grade, I played in a caddy championship along with guys from my high school. Just 13 years old, I beat all the high school kids. It didn't matter what clubs I had, I just picked them up and hit the ball. There were older guys that could hit the ball further, but when they'd get on the green, they didn't know what they were doing. But on the green is where I excelled. It's not how far you hit the ball, it's how well you hit the ball. I applied this same strategy into other areas of my life. It's the little things that need your attention because we so often overlook what the little things actually are. Your life as a whole is composed of little things day after day after day. And when you see them, you can start building the right foundation for who you genuinely are.

Golf is the only game I know where you penalize yourself. You're the only one you can blame for a bad shot. A game that is highly disciplined, and, yet, at the same time, you're out in nature's finest with all the sculptures of the fairways, the decision on the shot plane, and the thoughts that run through your head.

A lot of golfers tee up and go from tee to green. And when they're practicing on the range, they're heading for a flat line. So, when they hit a drive on the green, they get a downhill, side hill or uphill line. Then, they wonder why they have a bad shot. Well, from the range to the green, the circumstances have changed. I figured out my game improved if I played the game backwards, going from the green and figuring out where the flattest lines were. From flat line to flat line, I made a point to use every single club. The feeling of each club in my hands, their varying weights, I tried out every club in every different scenario. Life is like that, too. There are always a multitude of options and ways to do things differently in order to avoid mistakes and keep getting better.

At Catholic Central, we were state champions in football, track, baseball and all the popular sports. Golf was a minor sport. But I lettered for four years in golf.

In golf, you learn the difference between gamesmanship and sportsmanship. With gamesmanship, you play with other people's minds. I'd always play for a few dollars and then I'd beat them. And then when they gave me the money, I'd give it back to them. I never intended on keeping it, it was just fun to play for something.

My biggest accomplishment in high school was participating in sports. You can learn from sports because while you're competing you learn how to be a gentleman about it. Sports gave me the notion that if I worked hard enough, was disciplined and dedicated enough that I could do something with my life. When it came to golf, I knew I had whatever "it" was. It was within me, my own self-worth. I never bragged, but internally, golf helped me to build a foundation on which I could stand while overcoming adversity in other areas of my life. In golf, you're constantly faced with difficulty and lessons learned. And the accomplishment is being able to get through it, to stay in school.

In my senior year, I discovered that between Marywood, Mount Mercy and Catholic Central, there were over 500 awards in the black and silver room down at the city's civic auditorium. Lo and behold, I was in the top 5% of my class. Knowing this, it drove me to work harder. I wanted to be medalist. In my senior year at Catholic Central, my three other teammates and I shut out everybody, which was quite an accomplishment.

My short game broke the opponents' hearts, because they were always out there beating balls and beating balls and beating balls. The real game is from 100 yards. With other guys, they'd play from tee to green. I, on the other hand, would go from green to tee. The reason for that is when you're hitting balls on the range; you're on a flat lie. So, I would go from the green to the flattest lie to the flattest lie.

Golf requires a thorough-thinking process. You don't continue playing in a way that hasn't been working. Sometimes you have to go back and familiarize yourself with the same course over and over again. I had an advantage on the courses because I had caddied years before I ever played.

I would also play with my opponents' heads and create a game within the game. On certain holes that required a five iron, for example, I would pull out a three wood instead. They would, then, pull out their three woods and hit the ball 100 yards over the green. After they hit the ball, I put the three wood back into my bag and pulled out my five iron. But it was all received in good fun. They just laughed at my mischievous strategy.

Such an important figure in my life, my mother would come to watch me golf and she'd give me high-fives. Our high-five stood for the five letters T-H-I-N-K. If I'd leave the house, she'd give me a high five. That was her way of saying goodbye and reminding me, "Think before you do, don't do before you think." And that is the key to golf. You have to think before you hit the shot. More should go into the preparation for the shot than the actual shot itself.

Those who are best prepared are those who succeed. It isn't luck. It's never an accident. What's right for one person may be wrong for another. You have to know yourself and be true to what you know. All your aspirations and goals, you'll never know if you can achieve them unless you try. More importantly, you will never achieve them if you don't try. That's where we rely on innovation.

Golf prepared me for much more in life than how to hit a shot. The time I spent on the golf course was time I spent learning. Playing golf was one thing, but my time as a caddy was the most educational. Caddying for some of the more prestigious men and women in town, I had a front row seat to observe and learn from these skilled individuals. I made a point to absorb everything they did, even paying close attention to the way they carried themselves. As a bystander and a witness, I had the opportunity to choose which qualities I admired in each one of them, which qualities I wanted to have for myself.

Golf may seem to be a fairly straightforward sport, but it actually requires a lot of creative thinking. It's a game that teaches you how to manage adversity, and thinking creatively is how you do it. You hit the ball and then you must calculate how to handle the situation once it lands. In life, you make decisions, and similarly, you must calculate the best way to handle their consequences. These are the kinds of lessons I learned through golfing that helped me get ahead early in life. In high school, it was unheard of to make varsity your freshman year. But I did just that! Instead of the regular three stripes the other golfers wore when they graduated, I had four.

A minor sport when I was in high school, all of the other student athletes who played football, basketball, and ran would eventually ask me to help them with their golf game. That's because golf is a sport that doesn't involve injuries. It's a sport you can play all throughout your life. At my age, I no longer have the strength in my legs to play tennis. I can't play basketball because my eyes can't track the ball as it is passed rapidly around the court; and I sure can't play football. But, I can still golf.

The good players knew how well I knew the game of golf. They wanted me to caddy for them, because I would think for them. I'd align them and I'd give them the best club for each particular shot. I remember caddying for a gentleman who had a hard time breaking 100. He said, "What I wouldn't give if I could break 90."

I asked, "How much?"

He said, "Twenty-five bucks."

So, I lined him up and gave him the club. I did just about everything but swing the club for him. He shot an 88 in that game and I got 25 bucks. That was big money in those days. So, once again, it's all about giving. Give of yourself and someone else's life will be better.

I've never worked a job because of the money. I've always performed using best of my abilities, and people paid me to. I never demanded anything, and yet, today being retired, I had a plumber friend to come over to fix some issues in sink and some other household jobs. When I asked how much I owed him, he said that he didn't want any money because of everything I had done for him and everyone else in town.

I insisted that he name a price. He said, "Ten bucks." I gave him $20.

People remember those who give and those who take. It's the sin of self to consistently ask, "What's in it for me?" If you're greedy, you will end up being needy.

Golf inspired me to think selflessly instead of selfishly. It was also the reason Michigan State College recruited and awarded me a scholastic scholarship that paid for my books and tuition. To pay for my room and board, I worked odd jobs like clearing tables in my dorm. I was assigned to selling programs at football games, and one particular game, I had to guard the school's statue, Smarty, and so no one would steal or spray paint him. Throughout every job I worked and my entire career, I made a point to never tell myself that something wasn't my job. Whether a task was in my job description or not, if I was asked to do it, I did it to the best of my ability. The attitudes we choose to have determine everything—and attitude and gratitude come hand-in-hand. I appreciate my education and experiences, but it wasn't the classes I took. It was my involvement with the student body, with people, and the things I could do for them.

From each experience there is a lesson to learn. Attending Catholic grade school, Catholic high school, and originally a Catholic college, I was under the impression that everyone was Catholic. But when my golf scholarship took me to Michigan State, I discovered that was not the case. I thought, "Well, this is different." It's easy for us to become so wrapped up in our own familiar ways of thinking. Sometimes we just have to force ourselves to open our minds and realize there are other perspectives to consider in every situation. Very much like a game of golf, where the players must consider different angles and ways of taking a shot.

Every nation on this earth has its own unique problems. Some have a long history of civil war. Some countries suffer through incredible poverty. In some countries its citizens are forced to live under brutal dictatorship. In America, we have thick racial tension that affects everything we do. We've certainly come a long way, but we should be a lot further along by now.

Through business and caddying, I have watched the world change drastically over the years. The way we're going right now, we, the middle class are disappearing. Big corporations, big government, big banks control the lives of over 330 million people. They have the power and the money. If you have a brilliant idea and develop it into a company, a larger one will come along and buy you out. Sadly, people often sell their businesses for more money than they've ever imagined, and because they don't know how to invest and save, they invariably go broke. It's a vicious cycle—the way corporate America treats people.

If I had never golfed, I'm not sure I would have overcome most of my life's challenges. Golfing made me more observant; it forced me to make better decisions in life. And thanks to golf, I was able to afford college, become successful in business, and meet the needs of others.

I want you to think about your favorite activity, hobby, game, or sport that you enjoy. Now, please list below the necessary skills in order to participate in your activity.

____

____

____

____

What has your favorite activity taught you? For example, golf taught me think outside of the box, to consider multiple solutions to one problem.

____

____

____

____

What other areas of your life are these skills applicable?

____

____

____

____

How can you start TODAY applying these skills to other areas?

____

____

____

____

—Grand Rapids Press Photographer.

COUGAR GOLFERS TRIUMPH IN REGIONAL—Catholic Central, for the second straight year, has won the class A regional golf championship. Saturday, at the Grand Rapids Country club, the Cougars totaled 322 shots, one less than last year at Kent Country club. Left to right, Dan Pupel (82), Art Bott (81), Jim Sullivan (76) and Jim Black (83). Sullivan, with his 76, was class A medalist. East Grand Rapids won the class B title, totaling 336, and Comstock Park won in classes C-D, wit[illegible] a gross of 345.

Cougars Repeat Golf Triumph

Catholic Central, steady through-[illegible]t, won the class A regional golf [illegible]own Saturday at the Grand Rap-[illegible] Country club after South's [illegible]jans had thrown a real scare [illegible]he nine-hole point.

[illegible]th led all class A teams after [illegible] holes but faltered on the back [illegible]. The Cougars won out by [illegible] shots as Jim Sullivan totaled 76 for regional class A medalist honors. Art Bott had 81, Dan Pupel 82 and Jim Black 83.

East Grand Rapids led in class B, totaling 336 and Comstock Park was the classes C-D titlist on 345.

South, in second place with 330, was followed in class A by Ottawa Hills, 335; Union, 359; Grand Haven, 377; Muskegon, 379; Central, 398, and Christian High of Grand Rapids, which defaulted.

Top four clubs, Catholic, South, Ottawa and Union qualified for the state meet to be held next Saturday at the Midland Country club.

Dick Harrison was class B medalist with 80, Dale DeJong of Comstock Park taking the C-D honors with 79.

CLASS A.

Catholic Central (322)—Jim Sullivan 76, Art Bott 81, Dan Pupel 82, Jim Black 83; **South** (330)—Dick Meyers 77, Howard [illegible] [illegible], [illegible] Meyers 83, Tom Curtiss 88; **Ottawa Hills** (335)—Ron Laug 81, Tom O'Hara 83, Carlton Burt 85, Ted Grainger 86; **Union** (359)—Frank Skeeton and Fred Schwartz 81, Glenn Stuart 85, Tom Ziezini 112; **Creston** (369)—Norm Fleet 87, Dan Lipke 89, Harvey Bosely 96, Bruce Bowersox 97; **Grand Haven** (377)—Ed Suchecki 91, Charles Arnold 92, Ray Suchecki 96, Tom Murdick 98; **Muskegon**

Chapter Four

Journey as a Business Owner

Becoming a business owner was the farthest thing from my mind. I simply wanted to change positions inside the company for which I already worked. When I did, they never paid me the bonus for the new position that they had guaranteed me I would receive. That violation of trust set up the dominos that led to becoming my own boss.

When I started out in the corrugated box business, I worked for the Allied Corrugated Container Company. Consolidated Paper Company bought it out, and it became Consolidated Packaging. Originally working in sales and general management, I was promoted to general manager, where the company promised me a bonus. I went to all four of my managers and told them that whatever bonus the company gave me for that first year that I would split 25% of it between the four of them. At the end of the year, our division ranked most profitable in sales. Corporate said they would be giving me a raise, but informed me they weren't going to pay me the bonus that we had agreed upon. I felt betrayed and shocked.

I had to tell my managers that there was no bonus, and therefore no sum of money that I could split amongst them. And then I announced that I was going to resign. The company had proved untrustworthy. Without fax machines or any other modern-day ways of communication, I tele-typed a message to corporate and informed them of my decision to leave. It caused quite uproar. They all flew from Chicago to Grand Rapids and removed me from the plant. As soon as they did, I called the man who had originally hired me.

He was in Cleveland. I told him I was going to leave and start my own company. He said, "Hold on for a month because I'm going to come to Grand Rapids too. And between you and I, we can start our own company." And that is how Grand Rapids Packaging began.

Opening a small office on State Street, nearly 98% of those first sales were generated by accounts I had opened in the previous company. I hired other people to go in and service them so the customers who needed help would be able to contact me at the office.

One of my largest accounts happened to be Leon Chemical and Plastics. Jim Nicholas, who was president of Leon at the time, had purchased the Knap & Vogt plant on Richmond and Muskegon on the Northwest side of Grand Rapids. The previous owners had added a big warehouse in the back, and Jim said to me, "I'm not going to be using it. Why don't you?"

So, Mr. Sweet was able to purchase the finished goods. I was able to sell, and we used the warehouse as our distribution center. After working out of that location for a year and a half, we eventually built a plant of our own at 2700 Patterson Southeast in the eastern section of Grand Rapids, one block north of 28th Street. Nothing else was out there except this mound where we built the plant. That's when Consolidated Packaging brought their own general manager in and told us they were going to make sure that they put us out of business.

Truthfully, they were in a position to sell at lower prices than we could, but the 98% of those customers I brought with me stayed with me, and it's because of them that the old Consolidated Packaging plant closed and ours started to grow.

We went down into Schoolcraft south of Kalamazoo, and we put in two large plants there as it was on the railroad spur. At one plant, Wolverine Packaging had two corrugators, which combined the liner board and the medium to make the actual corrugated sheets. The large presses at that plant were capable of making big containers. The other plant there was called Automated Box. At Automated Box, the corrugated sheets became finished products. Not only could we slot and turn them into boxes and glue and finish them, but we also had the ability to rotary die cut at the same time.

After that, we were one of the only box companies to see the potential in Northern Michigan. The business traveled from Grand Rapids all the way up to Sheboygan. But the bulk of the business was from Traverse City, down. That's how Cadillac Corrugated Container not only serviced the companies in Cadillac, but it was also the hub for the entire northern region of Michigan because we were right in the middle of the customers we served. We were about 80 miles south of Traverse City, about 40 to 50 miles away from Lake Michigan, and going east, we had the upper part of Michigan. There were few people who wanted to spend the time and effort to work with those businesses, so they became an important part of our boxing industry too.

From there, we purchased and partnered with other corrugated box businesses. Mr. Sweet and I purchased Troy Packaging in Plymouth, Michigan. We purchased Design Packaging in Tiffin, Ohio. We became partners with a company out of Akron, and we purchased the West Virginia Paper and Pulp Company in Mechanicsville, New York—a paper mill that made fine papers and we could convert those machines over to liner boards, which are the faces of corrugated boxes, and the medium which is between the two faces.

With our partner in Akron, we successfully converted and brought in our feed stock of old corrugated boxes from New York and Boston. Our operations ran from a massive 600-acre mill on the Hudson River. We were the first U.S. Company to sell liner board and medium to Red China. That was when Nixon was in office.

By that time, James Nicholas's latest business venture wasn't doing well, so we merged his company with ours. Jim became president of Grand Rapids Packaging, I became Executive Vice President, and Mr. Sweet was chairman of the board until he sold his half of the company to me n 1978 and retired.

At that time, you could take advantage of losses with one company and utilize those tax benefits on the healthy business. That's when we got into plastics at 4050 Roger B. Chaffee, which became known as Grand Rapids Plastics. And underneath a holding company called AJAY Industries, we merged the trucking industry and real estate. We worked all these particular entities until our company closed due to the recession. In 1982, the prime rate of money you could borrow had risen from 21.5% to 25%, and people were no longer able to pay each other—and because people didn't pay us, we couldn't pay our bills and our company went out of business.

But whether I was getting paid or not, I still had debt obligations of my own. Interestingly, the buildings had been built by James Bowman, who was the president and owner of the Wolverine Building and who had built the buildings on Roger B. Chaffee.

Lo and behold, Jim Bowman came to me and asked if he could buy the building from which we'd run our plastics company. I happened to be handling the books for Sweet Bott Realty, so I gave him a figure that would not only pay Mr. Sweet's debt, but allow Jim to own the real estate. To my surprise, he asked me to accompany him to the closing when he bought 4050 Roger B. Chaffee.

After he bought out Mr. Sweet's interest, he put me down as a partner of his business at 4050. In other words, even though he owned the entire building, he gave me 50%. Of course, I would have to pay him back, but it gave me the opportunity to acquire some much-needed assets.

Around that same time, one of my bankers, William Broucek, was a friend of mine from the fifth grade at St. Alphonsus grade school. He suggested me to purchase the plastics company from the bankruptcy proceeding, which was the smallest entity I had then fresh out of bankruptcy. I could buy out Grand Rapids Plastics for $60,000, but I didn't have $60,000 because I had lost everything. I wasn't personally broke, but any profits from the business were paying my debts to the banks.

I couldn't believe it, but in 1982, Bill gave me $60,000. I didn't even have any collateral to offer him. So, I asked him, "Why are you doing this?"

He said, "Art, let me explain something to you. I don't loan money based on assets. I loan based on CHARACTER. And your character, alone, is why I'm behind you." He gave me the $60,000 to avoid pulling my loan. He even increased my line of credit, and within two years, I was able to invest in money markets. Then, two years later, I paid off Mr. Bowman. And now, I once again own Grand Rapids Plastics.

On the morning of June 27, 2001, my oldest son, Brian, went into St. Mary's for a heart cath. By noon, we were in the hospital chapel saying mass for the repose of his soul. The most difficult time in my life, I sold the business on September 11, 2001.

Exactly two years later, my oldest daughter was rushed to Ann Arbor in need of a heart transplant. But a mere three hours after the operation, Tami's new heart stopped beating. She was placed on the ECMO machine in intensive care. If her new heart didn't start beating within 72 hours, they were going to pull the plug and that would be it. The chief surgeon who had operated on Tami said that the chances were slim to none that she would survive. But Dr. Bartlett, who actually invented the ECMO machine, was there with me and said, "This machine will pull her through." I thank God for him every day because after 36 hours, her new heart miraculously started beating!

When she was brought her out of sleep, I started talking to her. Lying there on her left side, I grabbed my daughter's hand and said, "Tami, this is dad. Would you squeeze my hand?" And then she did. In fact, she responded to every question I asked her. But, we were not in the clear yet. Other issues began to surface. Hooked up to the ECMO machine, Tammy's blood had to be thinned. This was performed by removing the platelets, and then when her heart started beating, they replaced the platelets. This process typically causes strokes, and Tammy suffered four of them.

While they worked to stabilize Tammy there was nothing I could do. So I went downstairs to sleep for a couple hours. When I woke up, I rushed back to the intensive care unit, and there she sat, propped up in bed and smiling. "Hi, Dad," she said. Narrowly escaping death only hours before, her doctors said she had taken an unbelievable turn and was recovering well.

After Tami was better, I returned to work. Between 2003 and 2005, people were once again in need of work. And here, I had all these plants in the Grand Rapids area. I fixed them up and leased them successfully.

I noticed that within those few short years some peculiar things had happened. The inner city did not provide the poor and unemployed with effective transportation for, but new companies were building their factories out by the airport. This meant that the only people who could obtain these jobs were those who had cars. I knew something had to be done.

In downtown Grand Rapids, I went and spoke to the city officials there at Rapid Transit and an organization called Hope Network. I told them of the inner city's need for transportation to Kent Industrial Park, to 44th Street, and north in order to service my company and others in that area.

It wasn't an easy sale. Concerned that I was over-projecting the numbers, they didn't want to start such a program without proof that there was a need for it. I told them we have a responsibility to take care of people, reminding them that out of all the city's neighborhoods, it was perhaps the people in these areas who needed employment the most. There were employers ready to hire them, but the jobs existed outside their means of transportation. They needed the city's help. I suggested busses that would run on a schedule that accommodated their factories' work shifts.

At the same time, the 50-year-old Kent Industrial Park was deteriorating. During the period that Grand Rapids Plastics went out of business, I spent a great deal of money fixing up all the plants there, which once again, stimulated the owners of other plants to do the same thing. To further matters along, I asked the city of Wyoming to help find the money in their budget to resurface the streets and fix the curbs. To my surprise, they came to help. It was a community effort, but that idea had to be stimulated. It wasn't me. I simply recognized a need and provided the logic behind it.

After multiple negotiations between the cities of Wyoming and Grand Rapids, transportation from the inner city to the factories was achieved, and the streets, curbs, and sidewalks leading there were improved.

On September 11, 2001, Jesse Jefferson purchased the business of Grand Rapid Plastics. Two years later GMAC pulled their financing from Mr. Jefferson and closed the plant. On April 29, 2005, the name was reclaimed from the State of Michigan as Grand Rapids Plastics incorporated. Once I had everything ready to go, purchased certain equipment and got the plant cleaned and sparkling at 4220 Roger B. In 2007, the plant was finally up and running service orders for companies in Grand Rapids and short orders for others.

We had a large 1500-ton press. Lakeshore Diversified Products off the coast of Lake Michigan came over to see me with an order from one of their customers who needed large parts for the wheel wells inside the Chrysler Sebring trunk. They didn't have a big enough press, so they asked if I would work with them. I told them I would.

Chrysler sent up their quality person, Darrel Sukbar. Impressed with how the plant absolutely shined, Darrel asked to meet the owner. Originally I decided the ethical thing to do was to stay away from Chrysler. Chrysler was a customer of Lakeshore Diversified Products, who was our customer and the middle-man between us—without them, my company's needs and Chryslers would've never been met. But Sukbar insisted, and my son and co-owner, Jerry Art, Jr. convinced me to at least meet him.

"You really put something together here," Sukbar said. "Chrysler needs you." He invited my son and I to visit Chrysler. Prior to that visit, my son put together a PowerPoint presentation of my vision so I could present it to four of Chrysler's directors. After the presentation, one of the directors squeezed my right shoulder and in my right ear, he said, "You're a wise man. Welcome to Chrysler."

My first task with Chrysler was to tool for what was then the Chrysler model 200. Then, in 2008, Chrysler filed for bankruptcy. Here, I had built the business up with additional equipment and spent a great deal of money adding this equipment in order to accommodate their needs, and suddenly, there were no sales. And, so, from the time they went into bankruptcy to when they started up again in the state of Michigan, they had to pay me for the tooling because of something known as a mechanic's lien. Although Chrysler paid me for the work I had performed, I wasn't compensated for all the down-time, and regrettably,

I had to release some of my employees. The deal with Chrysler cost me three-quarters of a million dollars. I had to remind myself that this was just another one of life's hurdles, and it's why I'm here.

I'm not here to stare at my checkbook and admire all the money I have. I'm here to be my brother's keeper. So, in order to ensure that I could pay my employee's first and foremost, I borrowed money and I sold as much as I could part with.

Due to the rising unemployment in the country, I knew during the period that we were down that the federal government wouldn't allow Chrysler to go under completely, that it wouldn't let all these people lose their jobs. We knew Chrysler would inevitably make a comeback. So, I fixed everything up, and when Chrysler restarted production, we were back in business.

At the 2010 Super Bowl, Chrysler announced the 200 as the import car from Detroit, all the hard trim that was in that car and the 200 convertible came from Grand Rapids Plastics. We had all the resources they needed—the brick, the mortar, the machinery, the financing, and the sales. We took off. We had three shifts and more business coming in than ever.

Then, Fiat became involved with Chrysler. They stopped making the 200 and decided they were going to do everything in-house. Bringing in new people, the work we had been doing, they began to do themselves.

Although I was forced to lay off workers, I knew it was merely temporary. The new people Chrysler had hired were inexperienced, so I just sat back waiting for them to get in touch with me. When they did, I gave them a new quote based upon our experience, the parts, and what press they belonged to according to processing elements. Inevitably, we were hired.

They anticipated volumes, and at the same time, they specified a particular resin out of which they wanted us to make the parts. I was ordered to buy a truckload of it and purchase it myself. But during the processing of plastic, the size of the tool determines the required pressure. The tools they made were over-sized and we had to go almost three times bigger, meaning I had to use larger presses—meaning I had to raise my cost. Trying to get the prices out of Chrysler was really something. At the same time, the resin I had ordered for them didn't have the correct strength factor for the tools we used, so nothing fit. It was a comedy of errors.

It was good business, but Chrysler took up so much of my volume that I couldn't expand it. Then, Consumer Reports stated that the 200 Chrysler was the worst designed car in automotive history, killing 60% of my business. Chrysler blamed us for their failures, when in reality; we were not the recipient of what was going on down there.

Regardless, they closed their Sterling Heights plant, pulled all my tooling, and moved the 200 and the 300 to Mexico. The federal government gave a grant to Chrysler to change the Sterling Heights plant over to a truck plant with no regards to what the supply base and what we had endured. And so, my company went out of business.

When Chrysler pulled their business, Chemical Bank moved in and seized my assets. I had pledged too much, and in terms of the dollar amount about 90% of my wealth was taken from me.

These banks are ruthless. To this day, I'm still working through all that, so I can't give any results yet. But I do know this: America is not the country that it used to be. There are very few people worthy of trust anymore. It's been my experience that the people you can trust are the ones from the middle class. Because the middle class is here to serve—and working right alongside one another, all of us have jobs.

Here is a prime example of what I'm talking about. In 2013, I found myself in need of a kidney transplant. I was dying from polycystic kidney disease, which means I had cysts on my kidneys that made it difficult for them to filter toxins out of my body. It's an inherited disease. The strain can be traced to the Alcance Erin in Germany, which is the lower part of Germany and the upper part of France. Scott Harris who was a life donor of one of his kidney in his mid twenties introduced me to a lawyer, John Teeples, who had strong Catholic convictions. He helped me prepare my last will and testament. But because I was so weak, it took two weeks to complete the paperwork. And so, Mr Teeples took it upon himself to visit St. Mary's and find out if he could donate one of his kidneys to me. He was a perfect match. On December 9, 2013, at the age of 79, I was fortunate to be the recipient of a kidney from a live donor.

But it created more problems for me. Contracting the CMV virus, I was in and out of St. Mary's hospital for over four months. A couple of times they even lost me. But with the complete staff and Divine Intervention, I eventually pulled through. It's a marvel that I'm here. The last time I walked into Tom Maatman's office, a urologist I saw for prostate problems, he told me that I was a miracle man.

"What do you mean?" I asked.

He said I was the oldest ever recipient of a kidney at St. Mary's. I was three months away from turning 80, and everyone marveled. "Look at you, now," said Dr. Maatman. "God must want you to be coming back and to serve His people."

I said, "Well, if that's my calling."

"You're going to be a Centurion," he said.

"What do I do about that? I'm running out of friends." He told me to befriend younger people.

Hard times build inner strength. Our struggles make us wiser and help us to recognize our blessings. That time you didn't get everything you wanted, you survived. When circumstances were less than perfect, you survived that too. We need to shift our focus from our own needs to the needs of others. Build those relationships and forget about all the wants that are cluttering your mind and life.

Count your blessings for what you have. God gave you what you need. That's all you have to ask for. There are so many garage sales today because people are buying all this stuff they don't need. I've been asked many times, "Well, how do you make a million?"

I said, "Stop buying." That's all you have to do is stop buying. What do you need? You need relationships instead of substituting them with material items. I want to just talk to people. People don't talk to each other anymore. They text, they email. They like posts of Face book. But there is a concerning lack of real, face-to-face dialogue.

We have no choice in life but to play the hand we've been dealt. When you're down, the only way to look is up. God's grace and your own faith will get you through the tough times. God is always just, and things will always turn out the way that they should. I keep thinking about how nothing in life happens without an outcome. And, so, it is all a matter of attitude and gratitude. You can't give up. And once you make it through, you'll be thankful you found strength within your Higher Power. Hopefully, the pain I have overcome will help others to overcome their own.

We never know who is watching and listening to us. If you're a parent, your children are watching you. When you speak on the phone, your children are listening to you. All of this stuff is learned at home. When I caddied from the ages of eight to 18, I worked within three to four feet of some of the most powerful people in Grand Rapids. They let down their guards as they golfed, and I was there to hear and see them at their most natural. I gained experience from listening to them and asking questions.

From my business experience, I have learned to never consciously try to sell to anybody. Of course, I explained who I was and what I represented. But then I'd ask questions—and from the answers I received, I gave them what they wanted.

No one wants to be sold to, but most everyone is willing to answer questions. You learn through asking questions, and you will get answers to things you never even thought to ask. At my age of 83, I still ask questions, even of myself. Why am I here? I'm here to be my brother's keeper. And that's the most important part.

Through my whole life and in my faith, it's amazing the things that will come to light.

There's a verse in the Holy Bible that says a rich man making it into heaven is as likely as a camel walking through the eye of a needle. As my mother used to say to me, "Don't you get too big for your britches." These are the types of things you learn on your mother's knee. Having my mother at home, I think, was the greatest influence on my life. Nothing has ever surpassed the wisdom she imparted to me. I love to reminisce on our special high five and how she would spell "T-H-I-N-K" as her right hand connected with mine. “Think before you do,” she would say. “Don't do before you think.”

I realized that life is controlled by the Spirit within you. God is with you every minute of your life, 24 hours a day. If you are conscious of whom you truly are and of your purpose here, you will know that material things mean nothing. The most important thing, in my dying day, will be my name and my legacy. And that's all I'll take with me.

Sometimes we feel like giving up in life. But, it’s important that we stay strong and persevere because we never know what blessings are on the other side of our struggles. I have found more often than not that my circumstances are drastically better after hardship than they even were before it. I cringe to imagine what my life would look like today if I had given up every time a business endeavor failed or every time it looked as though I had run out of options.

What kinds of trials and hardships are you currently facing? Do you feel like you’ve run out of options?

Whether you do or don't, I want you to pay close attention to the exercise below.

Think of a time in your past where you felt similar to how you feel today. Perhaps you felt like your world was crashing down around you. Perhaps you felt like nothing would ever get better. Did things stay that way? Did things get better or worse? Please write out that experience below. Remind yourself of where you've been and how far you've come.

____

____

____

____

How are your current troubles similar to the one you listed above?

____

____

____

____

Can you think of someone you could reach out to for advice? Even if you don't heed their advice exactly, hearing another person's point of view can help you to spur new ideas you wouldn't have had otherwise. Below I want you to list three people whose advice you could seek. Name them and explain why they're a valuable resource.

Perhaps you aren't currently facing hardships. Maybe you're just stagnant in your life right now. Remember the metaphor of stagnant water in regards to change? Stagnant water is bacteria-ridden, dirty, and undrinkable. Right now, where are you stagnant in your life?

How could you make a change in this area?

Most importantly, what kind of change could you make in this area that would benefit others?

Chapter Five

Lifetime Achievement Award

When I was 79 years old, I received a Lifetime Achievement Award from Ernst and Young as entrepreneur of the 2014. A well-written nomination is required in order to be considered, and EY conducts a meticulous assessment of these nominations. If the committee is impressed with the written nomination, they will meet with the nominee for an interview.

While I was hospitalized, my comptroller at Grand Rapids Plastics, Rudy Feyer, submitted my name for the award. Still recovering from the kidney transplant, my son Jerry picked me up from the hospital and took me to

Grand Rapids for an interview with EY's committee. That day Friday, April 18—on my birthday.

I arrived at the plant just before noon in my hospital attire. To my surprise, the employees gathered to celebrate my birthday with me before the interview. I was in tears. I hadn't expected anything like that.

Due to the CMV virus, a urinary tract infection, and other health issues caused by kidney transplant, St. Mary's had already called after I was out for merely an hour and asked me to return in order to keep an eye on me. The committee was kind enough to agree to keep the meeting short so I could return to the hospital as quickly as possible. But they kept asking me questions, and so I kept giving them answers. Shaking their heads in disbelief of my obstacles and unlikely success, the interview ended up being almost three-hours-long. When the hospital called again and asked where I was, I finally had to excuse myself from the interview.

In June, I received a call from EY and they told me I was one of 39 finalists. Two from Grand Rapids, one of whom at Applied Imaging, two others from Northeast Ohio, and the remaining thirty-five were from Detroit. But Ernst & Young didn't know what to do with me. They had entrepreneurs for marketing, an entrepreneur for this, an entrepreneur for that, but they didn't have a category for me. They actually had to create one.

The ceremony for entrepreneur of the year was to be held on June 9, 2014. Hosted at the MGM Grand in Detroit, I was still weak but I attended anyway. I bought a table in the very front because I had to use a walker. I was surrounded by family and friends; even my sister from Utica was there. From St. Frances, I invited Father Jose Quintana, who had spent many nights with me as I recovered at St. Mary's. My kidney donor, John Teeples, was there. My brother and son attended. The day before the gala, Men's Warehouse whipped together a tux for me.

I rented a room at the MGM so I wouldn't have to travel so far without rest. My family did everything for me. They dressed me and my grandson, A. J. Bott III, put together a collection of photos of Grand Rapids Plastics for the ceremony.

I mentioned to my sister that the odds of two nominees from Grand Rapids and two from Northeast Ohio winning awards would be slim against the 35 from Detroit. I didn't know much about E&Y and the organization they ran, and they didn't know me either.

Paul W. Smith, the morning host from the radio station WJR in Detroit, attended the event and announced my award. He said, "We had a hard time figuring out what category to put this man, so we established a Lifetime Achievement Award in his honor. And it goes to Arthur Bott from Grand Rapids Plastics."

Strobe lights and LED lights lit up across the stage as I stood to my feet. Unable to walk on my own, I my brother took one arm and my son took the other. They carried me up the steps to the microphone. Weighing just less than 150 pounds, I was so sick and looked so old.

In front of about 600 people, there I was, Arty Bott, son of a beer truck driver, Mr. No Name. At one point in my life, I was the kid least likely to succeed. I was the one most people gave up on. Sure, I was friendly with my classmates and I got along with the girls, but it's not like I was ever class president or homecoming king. But our class president and announcer at Houseman Field College worked in the retail business after he graduated.

We can never know where life is going to lead any of us. It's our ability to change and adapt, and our spiritual determination that makes the differences in our adult lives. I was fortunate enough to have a mother who never gave up on me. I learned how to be strong from her. Every Tuesday, we recited the Mother our Perpetual Help devotions together—the Rosary.

Make a point of reflecting all the way back to where you first found your own identity. If you haven't yet, it's through the power of silence, prayer, and meditation that you arrive at the place you are destined to be. You won't find anything by turning on the television or starting at your cell phone. You must make room for the quiet time—time to talk with yourself and ask yourself questions. You need the peace and soundlessness of meditation and reflection.

As I looked into the crowd and my whole body relaxed, I thought of how far I'd come in my life. I was once a child with an inferiority complex who stuttered. It took years of hard work to transform into a person calm and confident. Stuttering wasn't merely just one problem within itself, it created all kinds of other problems too. Back then there was no such thing as speech therapy. I had to go through the trials and tribulations of having that disability entirely on my own. But it's amazing how most often it's the weakest part of your life that becomes the very example of strength you call upon for confidence later. In this life, we have to work for everything. Just remember, you always have the Holy Spirit in you. And God is with you, coaching you the entire time. When God calls, you better answer the phone. If you just listen, the Spirit will talk to you. But you have to be attentive. One of the best skills you can develop is listening to your conscious, to the Holy Spirit. The Life within you is the One you should listen to.

I have a difficult time reading aloud, and so my speech that night for the Lifetime Achievement award had to come to me on the spot. But I wasn't worried. I drew upon the strength of my past, and my speech rolled off my tongue as though I'd been a natural public speaker all my life. I think I spoke for nearly 10 minutes.

Struggling to speak, I'd go to the golf course and yell and cry. I had to endure the hurt, the will to live, and the will to overcome those things. I know that being alone on that golf course helped my golf game too. You have to be true to yourself and hang in there no matter how long it takes to get the results you desire. And if you find that you're going the wrong way down a one-way street, you better turn left or right and get out of the way of yourself.

I think the doubt we have about ourselves is natural. It's an inferiority complex, but at the same time, it's a warning sign. Sign that it's time to meditate, time to think, and time to get yourself on track. From there, you can build self-confidence, but only you can do it for yourself. It isn't something that is given to you. You must earn it. The power of the mind has been proven by many.

After my kidney transplant, I was looking up at my room's wallpaper there in St. Mary's Hospital and saw a facsimile of a cross. At the time, I was battling the CMV virus and I was weak. The virus caused awful shakes, and when they would take over I would just stare at that wallpaper and tell myself to let my mind go. I said, "I don't want to have spikes in my hands. I don't want to have spikes in my feet. I don't want to be gored in my side. I don't want to have vinegar instead of wine, and I sure don't want to have a crown of thorns." I would remind myself of how good things were instead of how bad I felt. I worked on my attitude, and in return, felt a lot of gratitude because

I had a lot to be thankful for. That's how I overcame the "poor me" syndrome during that time.

In life, they don't pass out a bunch of hankies. Misery loves company, and it's the company of a bunch of losers—to put it frankly. If you don't change your attitude, you too will become a loser. You have to want to go in the right direction. As a Christian, the ultimate success for which you should be striving as is the personal salvation of your soul. That's the final victory. And it has nothing to do with wealth or health. It's all attitude and gratitude.

I sure would like for my life to be an inspiration to those who are down and have given up. Right now, for instance, with the failure of the company, a lien on my home and the Small Business Administration waiting for my payments, things seem bad. But nothing will ever actually be as bad as we sometimes think they are. It might not turn out exactly as we hope, but one thing is for certain—one way or another, it will end. And however it does is what was meant to be.

We're all destined for something. It's why we're here. Even if your own parents say that you were an accident, I assure you they're wrong and you are not.

It's important that we stop lecturing and start encouraging. It should be so easy to read and to comprehend and to give hope and direction through your own tenacity. In other words, you need the perspiration with the inspiration. If you don't put your work shoes on, you'll never make footprints in life.

I didn't write this chapter in order to brag to you about my award. I want this chapter to inspire you to recognize validation when you receive it because sometimes we miss it.

Name a time you were validated. It can be as simple as someone telling you they appreciate you. It can be an award you won. It can be a "Thank You" card you once received. Name it and describe how it made you feel.

____

____

____

____

For what areas in your life do you think you should be acknowledged? Who do you think should acknowledge you for this/these thing/s?

____

____

____

____

Is it possible that they have acknowledged you in some way already? Think carefully. If so, how? If not, is it because you want to be acknowledged for doing things that serve your interest only?

____

____

____

____

In what areas of your life would you like to be acknowledged for? What steps could you take to make sure you receive this acknowledgment?

____

____

____

____

What kinds of things could you do for others that would definitely earn you validation and acknowledgment?

____

____

____

____

Local

WYOMING

GR Plastics owner earns lifetime achievement award

↓Article Part 1

By Justin P. Hicks
jhicks3@mlive.com

Arthur Bott has dedicated his life to others.

He raised his five kids as a single parent, continues to provide jobs for in the community and hasn't collected a paycheck since 2001.

But when the 80-year-old Byron Center man attended a gala earlier this month at the MGM Grand Hotel in Detroit, the spotlight was on him.

"So much of my life has been really spiritually driven and it's all about how you've helped people," said Bott, the CEO and chairman of Grand Rapids Plastics. "I'm humbled by the experience."

Bott was the recipient of the 2014 Lifetime Achievement honor, one of 10 Ernst & Young Entrepreneur of the Year awards handed out June 5 to business executives throughout Michigan and Northwest Ohio.

After hearing his name called, he was helped to the podium. Standing in front of the crowd, he ad-libbed an acceptance speech.

"I didn't have anything prepared and somehow, with the Holy Spirit, the words came out," Bott said. "I don't even know (what I said). ... I got a standing ovation and people said it was the finest speech."

THEME OF ADVERSITY

Grand Rapids Plastic CEO and Chairman, Arthur Bott, was recognized for his career of helping supply jobs to the less fortunate in the Grand Rapids area. (Joel Bissell/MLive.com)

↓Article Part 3

boxes for 25 years.

By 1982, however, the packaging company filed for bankruptcy, leaving him a 48-year-old single parent with no money.

"Who said it's easy? It's how you handle adversity," Bott said. "You don't learn one thing from success, it's fleeting. Every day, we've got to prove ourselves and overcome the humanness."

He persevered with the help of a few businessmen who took a liking to him,

↓Article Part 5

heart procedure at Mercy Health Saint Mary's.

Pressured to retire, and dealing with the grief of losing his son, Bott sold Grand Rapids Plastics. Less than two years later, the organization was bankrupt and its 200 employees were without jobs. Bott had not planned to rejoin the workforce after retiring, but seeing people struggling at the hands of a hurting economy, he felt a sense of duty.

Article Part 2

THEME OF ADVERSITY

Six months earlier, Bott has been suffering from a kidney disorder, yet there he stood on June 5, alive and in good spirits.

"I started to look into what my life has been," he said. "(You do that) when you've got a lifetime achievement award, and I never even expected something like that."

Bott grew up in a poor family. He started working at age 8 as a golf caddy, picking up paychecks in addition to golf and business talk from the people he assisted. After graduating from Grand Rapids Catholic Central, he attended Aquinas College before transferring to Michigan State University. He grew interested in business, namely packaging, and earned his degree in 1956.

After a short stint in the Army Reserve as a medic, Bott moved back to Grand Rapids and worked at Grand Rapids Packaging, where he sold corrugated

Article Part 4

who took a liking to him, and established Grand Rapids Plastics, a company that made replacement auto parts.

Hiring people from the inner city who otherwise would be in poverty was important to Bott, who said his purpose in life is to be his brother's keeper. He worked with the cities of Grand Rapids and Wyoming to adjust public transportation routes to stop at each of his five plants.

"We've got the jobs, and if you think (people in poverty) like entitlement, they just want the job," Bott said. "It's important to be loved, it's important to have something to do and something to look forward to. That's what they want.

"I'm here to help them make a living, and these people have never had a chance."

THE NEXT CHAPTER

Challenge struck again in 2001 when Bott's son, Brian, died during a

Article Part 6

my, he felt a sense of duty.

He began purchasing low-cost machines being sold at various auctions and cleaned up his old plants. Slowly, he rebuilt the company to a $40 million firm with about 300 employees.

One worker, 67-year-old Adele Hirkaway, returned from Bott's old workforce and plans to stick around as long as he does.

"(Bott) is my family and we always said if it came back up, we'd come back together, and we did," she said. "I'm a part of this company, so I am here all the time with him. When he retires, I'll retire."

Bott will tell you he "flunked retirement" and he does not plan on taking a second crack at it.

Why retire when you can restart a plant?

"Why should I?" Bott asked. "I've had so much fun doing what I'm doing. The gratification I get, the people's smiles and that we can all make a difference."

Chapter Six

Life and Church

Life is not about earthly things; it's about setting the proper goals. It's about striving for the ultimate success, a kind of success that life brings itself and reach heaven by leading a Christ-like existence.

I believe that we are created in the image and likeness of God. Living a Christ-like life preserves that image, and it will take us to eternal rest.

The image and likeness of God is the Spirit within you. That is why we must listen to our Spirit, because it guides us through life. The Spirit within us is what keeps us alive, but too many people choose to listen to false gods, the exterior stuff, and the material goods.

Materialism, self-satisfaction, drunkenness, these are the false gods. It started when Adam ate the fruit from the tree of life. We're all human and we all make mistakes, but we can't just say, "oh well," and leave it at that. We must attempt to minimize our sins, we must try harder every day—and when we do, the voices of all the false gods corrupting us will become weaker and quieter. One way to avoid sins is to focus on being generous and kind to others. You won't have time to sin if you're spending your time giving to those in need.

Remember the how the Bible likens a rich man getting into to heaven to the likelihood that a camel can pass through the eye of a needle? The only wealth one needs is the spiritual wealth you gain from giving. If you don't have the monetary resources to give, you can give of your time, you can lend a kind word and a smile. God provides everything we need in order to give.

As far as the material world is concerned, I do not consider myself a rich man. I have tried to the best of my ability to invest in heavenly riches by helping to improve the lives of others. Richness isn't what you have; it's what you can give away. The four Gospels detail Jesus teaching these basics during His life on earth. I have relied on these teachings since I reached the age of reason around the age of eight. For 75 years, I have practiced these basics and they haven't failed me yet.

Going to church keeps me in tune. I attend mass to receive the body and blood of Christ and to hear these teachings over and over so that I can continually be reminded how to keep them at the forefront of my heart and mind.

When I'm gone, I want people to remember me as a visionary and a doer. I've tried to be a thinker, but I'm no scholar. I just try to make things happen to the best of my God-given ability for the benefit of others. I am here to be my brother's keeper.

In some ways, I have achieved these goals. But, in other ways, I'm sure I've disappointed people. It happens. No one can please everyone, but most people will appreciate your efforts. With the best of my ability, I've always I tried to achieve "Thy will be done." In the end, it is all that is going to matter. And perhaps along the way, others will have learned the gift of giving as well.

Whether a person believes in God or not, everyone needs something to help ground them. If you haven't yet found a reliable way to ground yourself, that's okay, I'm here to help. First, we need to define what it means to be grounded. Grounding is basically just reminding yourself of what's important in life. When we aren't grounded, we tend to exaggerate the significance of things that don't really matter. Perhaps you become over-critical of your spouse and children. Maybe it's just a general sense of dissatisfaction and irritation. If you're not grounded, it can sometimes manifest as anxiety and panic disorders.

For me, attending church and playing golf are grounding exercises. For some, it's meditation. For others, it's volunteering, playing sports, yoga, or writing. What kinds of activities make you feel calm? An easy way to come up with this list is by thinking about how you feel *after* these activities. Do you feel energized? Optimistic? Do you feel like you have a clear, big picture perspective after any of these activities? Discuss below.

____

____

____

____

How do you want your grounding activity to make you feel? Be as specific as possible.

____

____

____

____

Does your grounding activity include other people? Do you think it should? Why or why not?

____

____

____

____

And finally, what are some other activities you could try for grounding purposes?

____

____

____

____

Chapter Seven

Making a Difference

Being involved with various charities and business endeavors over the years, the ideas I've had come from Divine Intervention. These kinds of ideas aren't something you can learn at school, they're something you're just blessed with. They involve having contact with your inner self so you can make a difference in the world around you.

Being in contact with your inner self isn't being self-centered. It's an intellectual conversation with the Spirit, and these ideas germinate from it. It's a kind of communication between the physical self and the spiritual self. It's what people call, "dancing to the beat of your own drum." It's the whole-self working together with the guidance of the Holy Spirit within you. There are smarter people than me in the world, but I have Divine Intervention to give me ideas that help others.

I have been able to use many my ideas in my businesses. But giving to charities and helping people in need are my favorite ways to use my ideas. I like to participate in the organization and promotion for these people and organizations.

A good example is when I attended mass at St. Frances one Sunday morning. It was raining, and the drops dripped from the ceiling onto my head as I walked down the aisle to find a seat. When I sat down in a pew, my pants became wet. I looked around during and after mass and noticed everything was falling apart. They had radiant floor heat, which circulated hot water underneath the concrete of the church. Traps regulate the zones throughout the church. During winter, your feet either felt like they were on fire because of all the hot-water going through the floor, or they were so cold because there was no heat coming from them at all. When I looked at the school parking lot next door, I noticed the heat radiating from the building.

After mass, I mentioned what I had observed and experienced that morning to Don Jandernoa, who headed up the St. Frances Xavier foundation for the school's repairs. We made arrangements to meet the following night to further discuss the problems. I devised a plan to start helping the church. First, I wanted to start a capital campaign so we could collect money that we would need for the repairs. I put Floyd Pierce, who repaired trucks as a profession, in charge of doing extensive research to find out exactly everything that needed to be fixed.

Don asked me to speak to the church and request the money from the congregation for the repairs. Here, I was once the kid with the speech problem and I was supposed to speak to an entire room full of people and ask them for money. I agreed to do it, but I didn't prepare a speech. I knew the request had to be genuine and unrehearsed. I allowed the Holy Spirit to serve as my guide that morning I stood in front of the parishioners.

The first thing I told them was that we needed a capital campaign to repair the church. I, then, asked them, "Who has a dollar? Will you raise your hand?" Everyone raised their hand. That was enough to start the campaign. The basket was passed around and everyone donated one dollar to our renovation fund that morning.

Every Sunday, I attended each mass and collected dollars. From there, the fund continued to grow until the renovation was complete. The final cost of the repairs was three-quarters of a million dollars.

After the church was completely restored, I paid to throw a celebration for the occasion. I contacted Ralph Hauenstein, Jr., who was in my graduating class at Catholic Central, to host a pig roast for us. We had two pigs, potato salad, beans, cole slaw, cakes and pies. The celebration welcomed all the church's members and the entire surrounding neighborhood.

Sister Winnifred was in charge of the choir, and I bought her the piano of her choice. On Holy Thursday, my kidney donor and his wife picked me up to attend mass at St. Frances. Still weak from the transplant and the other complications from surgery, Father asked the parishioners who marked the entrance to make way so that John could pull right up to the front door and I could walk straight in. I used my walker to make my way to the front pew.

When Sister saw me, she came to me like a flying nun. She pushed Father aside and announced to the church, "This man bought me my piano." I laughed as everyone hooted and hollered. Later on, I was a lay apostle at St. Jude's Catholic Church.

Art Kuiper, who was general manager of Tassel's Hardware over in Standale, invited me to play in a golf tournament with him. I had been so busy with the kids and my wife and other areas of my life that I hadn't played golf in almost 10 years. Nevertheless, I told him I would join him. I bought shoes, a bag, clubs, and everything else I needed. That tournament on Silver Lake.

I was over-par on the first two or three holes. Then, all of a sudden, it was just like magic coming out of a bottle. My skills kicked in. I finished the rest of the holes and ended up being the low man, winning the tournament even though I hadn't played for nearly a decade. That game prompted me to start golfing again.

Golf was a great way to earn money for charities. My wife volunteered with Healing the Children, an organization that brought children to the States from Mexico, Guatemala, and other poor regions of the world to get medical treatment and surgeries for various different ailments. Headed by Marva Donavan, one day she said to me, "We've got to pay these bills somehow."

Once again, I got an idea. I told her I would host a golf fundraising event to help her raise the money to pay the airlines, host families, and whatever else she needed money for.

Rotary International is an organization that similarly helps children, and recently I had formed Sunrise Rotary as a local endeavor. I put Rotary Sunrise to work, and with the help of a few other people, I set up the charity golf tournament. It was August, and we had to have the event by the end of the month, and so I called everyone I knew and asked them to get involved. Offering prizes to winners, one of those prizes on a particular par 3 was an all-expense paid trip anywhere in the United States. Starting my game on that hole, I outscored everyone and won the trip.

We gave prizes for ticket drawings as well. One prize was a plane trip to Puerto Vallarta, Mexico and a week's stay at the Marriott there. Shaking up the container, my wife pulled out a random ticket and we won that too! But because I had already won once, I told them to draw a different winner. Warren Reynolds, a sportscaster in town, was there as an emcee for the event and he won that trip. When the tournament was over, we had raised almost $40,000 to help Healing the Children

Golf became so much a part of my life that I had an idea for a golf course that was unlike any others in our area. Twenty-three of us from the city bought land and built what was to be the Thornapple Pointe Country Club. We then leased land from the county to put in a golf course. The public courses in the area weren't as challenging as some people would've liked. I wanted this golf course to be something that the average golfer who isn't a millionaire could enjoy and feel like they were playing on a first-rate course.

When the course opened, we had a tournament to raise money for another Rotary cause. I wanted to do it even bigger and better than before, and so I suggested, "Let's have a four-man scramble in the morning, and in each foursome we will have a pro play with us." I offered $1,000 for first place, $500 for second, and $250 for third. In the afternoon, we had a five-man scramble without a pro.

For the event, we had a big tent, ice carvings, chamber music, and the works. It looked like a wedding reception. A teammate of mine, who is now passed away, Jim Black, called me up the day before. He asked if he could put together a foursome as well.

Everyone came out. Jim Black was a partner with Jim Sullivan who owned Sullivan's Riverview Furniture and some of the Days Inns too. In the second 18 holes, they called and said Jerry Shoemaker, who was in their foursome, had skulled a drive. To skull a drive means that the ball didn't lift more than three feet off the ground and bounced and bounced and bounced and bounced. Lo and behold, it went into the cup for a hole-in-one and Jerry won a Buick Century for that hole. Ironically, he had just purchased a Buick Century the week before. We continued helping Healing the Children charity. We brought in the children with cleft palates or heart problems or whatever medical issues they had. We raised money to help host families care for not only the children, but their parents too. We helped defray some of the costs by raising money to be used wherever it was needed.

When I moved to my home in Byron Center, I attended St. Sebastian church. There, I was involved with Monsignor Gus Ancona and the restoration of his rectory, the restoration of the hall, the restoration of the church, and I was on the pastoral council for the building of a new, larger church at St. Sebastian.

The foundation I led at St. Sebastian proved to be instrumental. Working with the art committee, the large circle of colorful, leaded glass was split into quarters and hung over the main altar. Few people know that the colors used in it are the colors of the vestments that were used during mass.

Monsignor William Duncan asked me to pay for a statue of St. Sebastian. I used money from my foundation to pay for the statue. I have invested what I could afford and have made sure all kinds of different people have been helped through the foundation. Still in existence, the foundation continues doing charitable work.

The American Legion and the American Red Cross needed a host for a Russian couple and their son who had a hole in his heart. He had an operation in Russia that failed, so they brought him here for a different surgery. I volunteered to host that family.

When they stepped off the plane, all they had was one flight bag, nothing else. I bought them toiletries, anything I could think of that they may need.

I owned a Russian translation book which I referenced all day to communicate with them for those three months they stayed with me. Through our conversations, I discovered that the father was a judge and made only $35 a month. The mother was a legal secretary and made $25 a month.

Through donations, the family received $25,000. The father offered to pay me back for my contributions, but I didn't want his money. Instead, I asked him to edge the grass along the driveway and curb with my electric edger. Later that day, I received a call from the police. The father had taken a saw to the concrete all the way down the street and up another street. The neighbors had called the police reporting a strange man on his hands and knees sawing along the side of the road. I explained the situation to the police, who passed along the information to my neighbors.

After my neighbors found out about the Russian family and their hardships, they donated clothes to them. Everyone came out to the house and packed their donated items in boxes from my corrugated box business. Then, he used the money to ship that stuff back to Russia.

Just recently, when I retired from business, I found myself working in Hospice and for those with particular needs. I also work with individuals affected by dementia, those who are lonely and elderly. I understand what they're going through. I am 83 years old, and I've already buried one son, many of my friends from Catholic Central, and two of my teammates from the Rotary golf tournament, Jim Black and Jim Sullivan. Growing old is a bizarre, different phase of life, and so too it comes with different needs.

My personal CPA has been affected with diabetes, gout, and kidney disease. I spend a great deal of time with him. He's coming around, but is still quite ill. In my age group, there are plenty of people who need help. Most of the people my age aren't in a position to be the helpers and the givers anymore. It's my greatest privilege to be able to help them at my age.

Instead of hiring a name brand landscape company to work on my lawn, I support two Guatemalan men to work with me on my yard.

I've been in the building business. As a general contractor, I designed and built my own home. I selected all the people who fulfilled my ideas. Because of them, my home was named West Michigan Cosmopolitan Magazine's Home of the Year in 1994. I've been in the mortgage business, assisting people to arrange their mortgages. I was in the heating, cooling, and sheet metal business, helping people who needed financing for these things too. I've also been in the self-serve and automatic car wash business. The first one I opened in Texas Corners in the suburbs of Kalamazoo. The second one was in Spring Lake. The third one was in Hudsonville on Highland Drive. Another one was off from Kalamazoo between 60th and 68th. I sold all but one, and that one's in Battle Creek. It has seven self-serve bays and one automatic.

I've been in the lending business, where in the late 90s, I was invited to help people who needed money for home renovations in order to flip houses. It was a thriving business up until the housing bust. I think I had at least 45 homes in that portfolio. During the boom, the people who asked for money already had permanent financing in place once they were completed. But during the housing crisis, the mortgage companies collapsed. Since the mortgages weren't there, I was forced to finish the homes off myself and ride that through.

Regardless of the reasons my businesses ended, I started them as a way to help people with their needs. The large corporations, the large banks, the large automotive companies and technology have been eliminating jobs throughout the last few years.

We're only allotted so much time in this life, and when that allotment runs out, there's no such thing as borrowing more. Be aware of each day you have, and do the best you can according to God's will. Think simple. Think in the terms of "Thy will be done," not in terms of your own personal will. The will of God urges you to find where and how you can give, not look for ways to receive.

The wants of life have to be through your own effort. You're not entitled to wants. You have to work for those. But we all have basic needs as human beings, and we the people that own the country should furnish the basic needs for others instead of supplying ourselves with wants. If you need transportation, for example, you can buy an economic vehicle or take the bus. If you want to be really thrifty, you can ride a bike or walk. There are many different types of inexpensive transportation.

These are things we really must conquer each and every day before we lose sight of what we are and of our own identity. Society is having an identity crisis. Most people don't know where they are or where they're going. They're lost. That's why I think, today, there is so much alcoholism and so much drug abuse.

I have never seen the cause of death in an obituary to be from hard work. All I know is that something stopped working. If you don't use it, you'll lose it. And that's why death comes early for so many people. They stopped using their God-given gifts.

All of these things are so simple. It's common sense. It isn't what we do and what we say, it's how we communicate with our families and our friends and help each other along the way. We must stop judging people by their grade point average, their athletic abilities, or how much they own. We've lost our way because we glorify people who have accomplished something in a very short period of time. But we don't glorify the honest, good people out there who don't have their names etched into buildings. So many live productive lives, so many are following the lead of what Christ came on earth for—to be our brother's keeper.

Being an entrepreneur is about giving until your service is no longer needed. An entrepreneur is a visionary who follows his or her vision and tries to put that vision into reality so they can continue helping others. The entrepreneur goes into the unknown. They're the ones who know they can succeed without hiring others to do it for them.

We're a nation of entrepreneurs. Just look at the country we have. We're a young country, and everyone's burning desire is to work for themselves. You can look up and down the line. They all want to be recognized through their stores or whatever it is that they do. They're meeting people, and they want to be a part of something. And that's what an entrepreneur is. They're catalysts bringing people together for a common purpose. It's a great way to use your Divine gift.

I want you to think about stewardship versus ownership. "Ownership" means that one is "free of any encumbrances or limitations." When you own something, you answer to no one regarding your possession. And this is exactly why I've preferred to think of my businesses as forms of stewardship. Merriam-Webster defines "stewardship" as "the careful and responsible management of something entrusted to one's care." Even as a homeowner, if the taxes aren't paid, you'll find the owner of your house is really the county you live in. All you're doing is paying the bills. In reality, we own nothing. And if you're following God's will, know that you don't own the plan and blessings He has planned for your life. You are a steward of these things. God trusts you to responsibly and vigilantly care for the responsibilities He has placed in your hands—and that includes His blessings, too.

So, think back to when you listed your talents and how you could use them to help others. God gave you those talents. He made you the steward of those skills. Doesn't that make you feel good? When we are trusted with responsibility, it makes us feel special. Child psychologists and other pediatric professionals recommend designating chores to children because when they complete them they feel proud, accomplished, and praiseworthy. Likewise, we are children of God and we can know that we are loved by Him because He has entrusted us with our individual talents and skills.

The Following Pictures Are From The West Michigan Cosmopolitan Magazine When My House Was Featured As The Home Of The Year. And Recently Featured On A Television program As A Home Built 24 Years Ahead It's Time.

Chapter Eight

All I Want

My whole life has been about helping people, so when I was asked why I wanted to write this book, I had to think back over all 83 years of my life, what I've learned, and how it could all help others like you.

My first life lessons were delivered to me through my family's poverty. Growing up poor meant that I had to work from a young age and I had to work hard. I watched my parents struggle, and while it was due to the country's overall economic situation at that time and through no fault of their own, i.e., the Great Depression, I knew that I didn't want to struggle like they did.

I sought out people who were at a place in their lives like where I knew I wanted to be someday. I observed them. I humbled myself, asked questions, opened my ears, and learned from them. I want you to consider the goals and dreams you have for your own life. Now, can you think of anyone who embodies those things? Even if they're not doing *exactly* what you hope to do, think of a person or group of people who at least possess the characteristics you'll need to get to where you want to go.

List the people who would be beneficial for you to pay attention to, observe, and learn from:

____

____

____

____

Where are they? Where do they hang out? Where do they work? What social groups/organizations do they belong to?

____

____

____

____

In the space below, come up with TEN different questions that would be useful to ask them?

Is there anything preventing you from joining their group/s? If not, name the first THREE steps you need to take in order to make contact with them. If there are realistic things preventing you from joining them, name the first THREE steps you need to take in order to overcome those obstacles:

When I was a child, I suffered from a terrible speech impediment. I stuttered so much that it was not only embarrassing to talk to people, but it was just plain difficult. I spent the majority of my time alone. Because there wasn't any kind of speech therapy available to me at that time, I spent my solitude practicing to talk without a stutter. But perhaps even more importantly, I learned how to be my own best friend.

Are you able to consider yourself your own best friend? My best friend is me, myself and I. If you had a friend who spoke to you the way you speak to yourself, would you stay friends with that person? If you have a bad habit of negative self-talk, probably not. Now is the time to change those bad habits. There is no greater favor you can do for yourself than becoming your own best friend.

List FIVE ways in which you are NOT your own best friend:

____

____

____

____

____

____

List FIVE ways you can start to be your own best friend TODAY:

____

____

____

____

Most likely, I would not be the person I am today if I had never started golfing. Not only did I enjoy playing golf, but I was good at it, too. I stuck with it, and it helped me build the self-confidence I so badly needed in my younger years. It may just sound like a simple sport, but I also learned countless lessons from playing golf that were applicable to other areas in my life.

What sports/games/hobbies/arts/crafts/activities do you enjoy?

____

____

____

Are you good at it/them? If yes, list FIVE ways it/they make you feel. If you don't consider yourself to be very good at it/them, list FIVE ways you can improve:

____

____

____

____

____

____

In my professional life as a businessman, I always made sure to do right by my clients. I went out of my way to go above and beyond what my clients expected from me. And I never took on a business I thought wouldn't help other people—I *only* went into businesses where I knew I could help other people. Now, think about your own career.

How do you make sure you're "doing right" by your clients/boss? List THREE ways:

____
____
____
____

Do you go above and beyond the expectations of your clients/boss? If so, list FIVE ways you can rise even higher. If not, list FIVE ways you can make a change and start TODAY:

____
____
____
____
____
____
____

Are you currently in a business and following a career path that will help you help others? If so, how so? If not, how can you change that?

____
____
____
____

Finally, I want you to think about life and all its unpredictability. Whether it was my fault or not, many of my businesses failed. Things don't always go as we plan.

Unexpected obstacles are always hiding around the corner, people change, our environments change, the landscape of our professions change. We can't control everything; in fact, we barely have control over anything. But we *do* have control over ourselves. No matter your occupation, whether you're in business like me or you're a stay-at-home mother, few qualities are more important than our ability to be flexible.

Think of a time in your life or career when circumstances changed unexpectedly and you were able to be flexible. What happened? How did that work for you?

____
____
____
____

Think of a time in your life or career when circumstances changed unexpectedly and you were NOT as flexible as you should have been. What happened? How did that work for you? What could you have done differently to improve your situation and make for a better future?

____
____
____
____

List FIVE ways you can be more flexible in the future

____

____

____

____

____

____

I hope my life story has inspired you to live your own best life. Life is complicated and strange at times, but it's a beautiful thing we must never take for granted. If you learned anything here, I hope most that you learned to answer when God calls, to rely on Him for direction, and submit yourself to His will. These are the three things that will always work and will always lead you to success. That's what God wants for you. He wants you to be successful so you can give him the glory and share your testimony with others, just like I have done here. NEVER GIVE UP...NEVER GIVE UP!

About Art Jerome Bott Sr.

BUSINESS

Grand Rapids Plastics Reopening

Founder and CEO • January 30, 2007 to 2014 • Grand Rapids, Michigan

Grand Rapids Plastics

Founder and CEO • January 30, 1982 to 2001 • Grand Rapids, Michigan

Grand Rapids Packaging

President and Co-Owner • January 30, 1968 to 1982 • Grand Rapids, Michigan

Consolidated Packaging

General Sales Manager • January 30, 1957 to 1968 • Grand Rapids, Michigan

EDUCATION

Michigan State University

Class of 1956 • Business and Engineering • Packaging Engineer • Bachelors of Science • East Lansing, Michigan

Aquinas College

1952 to 1954 • Engineering Science • Grand Rapids, Michigan

Catholic Central High School

Grand Rapids, Michigan

"Art Bott Lifetime Achievement Awards Speech"

Life is not about ownership, is about stewardship. I woke up one day and found out that instead of being in the stock market, I was investing in my city. Pope St Francis says to feed the poor, and that's what we have done. We build a business around the poor; we were able to get the rapid transportation system from the inner cities to be able to offer transportation to the people who wanted the jobs but didn't have a car to get to it. All I can say is that we currently employ more than 300 people, they are not broken they just need help. We must find means to help the poor, and not just pass money.

The most important question of the night is; why are you here, we are here to be our brother's keeper. The only thing we bring with us to our final days is our name. Everything else we leave behind, and what are we going to leave behind?

We can help by supplying jobs to those who are employable but don't have jobs, work with the churches, and organizations that provide the means for those who don't want handouts, they want opportunities.

"Character is etched into Beauty by the daily discipline and duties done." ~ Arthur Jerome Bott Sr.

Made in the USA
Lexington, KY
06 July 2018